SHREWSBURY
PICTURES FROM THE PAST

SHREWSBURY
PICTURES FROM THE PAST

Toby Neal & Phil Gillam

First published in Great Britain in 2001 by
The Breedon Books Publishing Company Limited
Breedon House, 3 The Parker Centre, Derby, DE21 4SZ.

ISBN 1 85983 255 5

Printed and bound by Butler & Tanner, Frome, Somerset, England.
Jacket printing by GreenShires, Leicester, England.

Contents

Acknowledgements

Most of the pictures used in this book have come from the archives of Shropshire Newspapers. However, we are grateful for the following who have also kindly given permission for the use of their photos: Stan Turner, Ray Farlow, Shropshire Records and Research Centre, Rita Beddows, Peter Shone, John Powell, David Trumper, Bryan Thorne, Brian Rowe, Roy Pilsbury/Greenhous Group, Pete Kelly, Sid Rowlands, John Barker, S. Foley, Vernon Carter, Derek Pugh.

Introduction

Built within a majestic horseshoe bend of the River Severn, the historic heart of Shrewsbury has been – for the most part – protected from the sort of large-scale 20th-century redevelopment that has so changed the character of many other old towns.

Indeed, so tightly is Shrewsbury held within the embrace of the river that when the Normans arrived to fortify the town, all they really had to do in terms of protection was build their castle on the thin neck of land which was the only viable way in. Thus, Shrewsbury became virtually an island.

Its development over the centuries was natural, organic. Even in the faster-paced modern era, the odd building here and there may have been replaced from time to time (and of course there are some notable examples!) but these were specific modifications without the cataclysmic changes that dual carriageways and insensitive planning departments have been known to unleash elsewhere. And Shropshire's proud county town, therefore, is today not only rich in Tudor buildings and other architectural gems that reflect its gentle growth through the ages, but it also still boasts an intricate medieval street layout connected by a network of charming 'shuts' and passages.

I would not wish to give the impression that Shrewsbury has been immune to progress or the shifts in architectural style and fashion. Not a bit of it. The town has buildings and 'street furniture' representing every era. Of course some change is for the good and some – on the other hand – is damaging.

In living memory – and regrettably as far as many of us are concerned – more than 50 of the town's historic buildings have been torn down and replaced with concrete and glass. But Shrewsbury has still been very lucky, compared to some places, in retaining so much of its beauty and heritage.

A corner has been turned now. People are much more aware of how precious our old buildings are. Everyone understands the concepts of preservation, conservation and environment. There is an ongoing dialogue between concerned townspeople about how Shrewsbury should now move forward without destroying any more gems. This greater appreciation has to be a good thing.

Meanwhile, in this book, we do not attempt to take in the great sweep of history that Shrewsbury represents – although we nevertheless hope that the spirit of the town shines through. Here, we merely look back over the decades within living memory, presenting photographs mostly from the second half of the 20th century, hopefully evoking fond memories for many older readers while intriguing and delighting younger ones too.

The majority of the photographs come from the Shropshire Star's massive archive and from the Shropshire Newspapers collection. Since the *Shropshire Star* was not born until 1964 a good number have been 'begged or borrowed' from other sources. We thank all those who have been good enough to let us use these wonderful images.

Phil Gillam

A Changing Townscape

Towns have to change. It would be a strange world indeed if every lamppost, every litter bin, every telephone kiosk and every shopfront remained untouched from one generation to the next. It would be like living in a museum. But looking back over recent decades perhaps some 'modernisations' are to be regretted.

In Shrewsbury, as in towns up and down the country, irreplaceable structures, some proud, often highly elaborate buildings of real character and elegance, have been bulldozed to be replaced by the bland and the utilitarian.

In Shropshire's still lovely county town there are a handful of striking contrasts we can look at straight away. Goodbye Raven Hotel, hello Woolworths. Goodbye Crown Hotel, hello Crown House office block. Goodbye George Hotel, hello modern, functional retail outlet. Goodbye old Shire Hall in The Square, hello Princess House. Goodbye Victorian Market Hall, hello 1960s Market Hall. Five huge changes bang in the heart of historic Shrewsbury. And many would say five huge mistakes. All of these changes, incidentally, are vividly illustrated in this book.

Consider for a moment how much more of a tourist magnet Shrewsbury would be today if these replacements had never been allowed. In this opening section, though, we'll look at selective demolition in the Victorian suburb of Castlefields, the creation of a new fire service headquarters, the old Priory Boys' School before it was transformed into the Sixth Form College, the long since gone railway station in Abbey Foregate, Smithfield Road in the 1930s, the railway locomotive sheds in Belle Vue, and a sadly neglected Howard Street Warehouse before it rose again as The Buttermarket.

It is all too easy to dwell upon what Shrewsbury has lost in recent decades. Yet there is so much to celebrate, so much to cherish. Perhaps most tellingly, the spires of Shrewsbury's fine centuries-old churches still dominate the extraordinary skyline and can be viewed from miles around. The town still has more than its fair share of beautiful buildings and atmospheric streets. It is an exceptional place.

And there is great hope now that a much more sensitive approach by town planners and property developers will, in the years ahead, demonstrate proper respect for Shrewsbury's rich history and splendid architecture. High quality conservation on the one hand and thoughtful new development on the other must surely be the way forward.

The future looks bright.

Shrewsbury General Post Office on the corner of St Mary's Street and Pride Hill in the 1920s. It also housed the automatic telephone exchange. The car on the right is probably a Humber. The photographer must have used a very slow shutter speed – note the ghostly image of a car outside the post office entrance.

The decorative pointed top to the tower at the Eye, Ear and Throat Hospital is removed in November 1959. It was taken down because it served no purpose and it was cheaper to remove it than repair it. The hospital closed in January 1998. After over 40 years away, the tower top made a surprising comeback in 2001 – a new version was erected as part of a scheme to turn the building into flats.

It's 1965 and perhaps these toilets in historic Butcher Row were considered fab, gear and groovy by the planning department of the day. Had they been constructed alongside contemporary sixties buildings like Telephone House on Smithfield Road or the new Shirehall in Abbey Foregate then hardly an eyebrow would have been raised. But surely one or two more sensitive souls must have disapproved of these modern loos going up alongside historic gems like The Bear Steps and The Abbot's House.

Because the new fire service headquarters in St Michael's Street were built on low level land alongside a main road they were curiously unobtrusive and so the architecture did not clash with its immediate surroundings. Here, in this 1970 photograph, we see the final stages of the '£110,000 fire headquarters' taking shape.

The abandoned part of the Shropshire Union Canal at Ditherington was being emptied into the River Severn in September 1945. As it emptied, the rubbish thrown in over the years became visible. The homes on the left are Wingfield Close, with the long-disappeared Spring Cottages on the right. In the distance is The Comet Inn, which is now called The Coach.

View from the tower of St Chad's Church in 1950, with the 1869 Market Hall and clock tower on the left, with centre, the former County Theatre and cinema, which was about to be converted into Astons furniture shop. The round structure just visible between the market clock and St Mary's Church behind it is the old water tower.

Not a country house at all, but the rather grand offices of Furrows, the Ford car dealership in Coton Hill, Shrewsbury, pictured in the late 1930s. Of course the building has a history. It is in fact Benbow House, the birthplace of Admiral Benbow, the 'Nelson of the 17th century'. For a while in the 19th century, the building was used as St Mary's Vicarage. Then, in around 1910, Mark Davies, who had a garage on Dogpole, opened another branch of the business in the garden of this fine house. This was called the Shrewsbury Garage Motor Works and was in turn bought, in 1919, by Cyril Harrison-Watson, who had set up the Furrows company a year earlier. There has never been a Mr Furrow. The name comes from the furrows ploughed up by tractors used by Mr Harrison-Watson for a government food production scheme during World War One.

This picture of the railway station forecourt must date from before 1901 because it was in this year that a lower storey was added to the lovely Victorian frontage of the station. Massive excavations were needed to make this possible. The striking memorial (erected in 1874) commemorating distinguished 19th-century surgeon and MP William Clement was later moved, firstly to The Dingle in the beautiful Quarry Park, and then to a much less prominent position, a quiet, leafy corner near the Greyfriars Bridge. Campaigners have, of late, been calling for complete restoration of the obelisk which for many years was sadly neglected, its stonework defaced with graffiti and covered in moss and mould, its four fountains rusted and broken. Whatever would Mr Clement have said!

At first glance, just another garage in Abbey Foregate, photographed here in 1969. But in fact the frontage disguises a medieval building which has miraculously survived the changing fashions of the centuries.

It's 1974. Rubble, wide open spaces, and a boarded-up Morris & Co corner shop at the top of North Street. These help tell the story of what turned out to be only partial redevelopment at Castlefields. Bright new homes were to follow. But the much more romantic Victorian streets did, in the main, survive. As did wonderful little pubs like The Canal Tavern and the Dog & Pheasant.

Rowley's House around February or March 1937. Its beauty had been brought to light by a 'slum clearance scheme' which destroyed many old properties around it to create an inner loop road to ease the town's traffic congestion. Rowley's House was turned into a museum to house Roman relics found at the Roman city at Uriconium. It opened as such on 7 April 1938. A one-way traffic scheme for the town came into operation on 1 August 1938.

The Priory Boys School in 1968. Today the building houses Shrewsbury Sixth Form College.

Rowley's Mansion in Hills Lane in the 1920s. It was used as a warehouse by R.A. Downes and Sons, including for wool and haberdashery. They had two green vans which made deliveries all over Shropshire and to a large part of Wales. The buildings on the right were demolished around 1935.

This site bounded by St Austins Street, Bridge Street and Lower Claremont Bank, seen here in about 1960, was given planning permission for a six-storey car park to accommodate 430 cars.

Work gets under way in February or March 1962. This photograph makes an interesting comparison with the previous view. The chimney in the background was probably part of the Morris's bakery complex, which is now the site of the Academy nightclub.

Almost there… The new multi-storey nears completion in June 1963. The NCP car park was permanently closed at the end of October 1998 because it was beyond economic repair.

General Sir Bernard Paget, an old boy of Shrewsbury School, unveiled the school's war memorial on Sunday, 25 July 1948. The ceremony was attended by pupils, old boys, and next of kin of the fallen. The memorial took the form of a marble wall bearing the names of the dead. Afterwards school buglers sounded the *Last Post* and wreaths were laid by Sir Bernard, headmaster Mr J.F. Wolfenden, and head boy D.L. Shaw.

The long-gone Shrewsbury Abbey railway station. The Potteries, Shrewsbury and North Wales Railway, which was later revived as the Shropshire and Montgomeryshire Railway, ran from here and also had a little station at Meole Brace (hence: Station Road in the old village). The enterprise was perhaps at its busiest during World War Two when its wagons transported ammunition from Nesscliffe.

Owen's Passage in Castle Street in 1960. Church Farm Café, a popular post-war venue in the heart of the town, was in a 13th-century building. It was originally a large hall which was turned into two cottages in medieval times. It was destroyed when the 1960s Littlewoods and Woolworths development took place.

The quite splendid Castle Gate Congregational Church at Coton Hill in the 1950s.

This pretty view of Barrack Passage, off Wyle Cop, has hardly changed at all.

The terribly pessimistic caption writer who put words to this picture in 1969 asked: 'Could this lovely view of Shrewsbury Square soon be a thing of the past?' He spoke of plans already approved for the demolition of the old Shirehall and a scheme under way for a complete new look for the Square. Okay, he was right about the Shirehall (to the right of this view) which was pulled down in 1971 (a crying shame), but thankfully this scene is pretty much the same now as it was then.

This corner unit at the junction of Butcher Row and Pride Hill has undergone many transformations. Here it is in December 1970 as The Golden Egg restaurant. Notice also the lovely old chemist shop to the right.

Summer 1953 and preparations are under way in The Quarry for Shrewsbury's famous Flower Show.

Tatty and abandoned, the old British Legion Head-quarters in March 1969.

Part of the Royal Salop Infirmary was evacuated in 1959 after a landslip behind the hospital. This was the scene on 2 September when wooden frames and timber shoring were being used to try to avoid further subsidence.

One of the last patients is moved out of the Royal Salop Infirmary on 20 November 1977. Fifty-two patients were transferred to the new Copthorne General Hospital, the eight ambulances completing the operation in two and three-quarter hours. The official opening of the new hospital was almost a year later, on 17 November 1978, by Prince Charles. It was thereafter called the Royal Shrewsbury Hospital. The RSI was later developed into a parade of shops.

A pleasant 1930s view of Whitehall on Monkmoor Road. Today, like its London namesake, it houses government offices. But it is in fact the grandest Elizabethan private residence in Shrewsbury. It was built around 1580 by Richard Prince, a lawyer, using stone from the monastic part of the Abbey. As red sandstone is likely to deteriorate quickly, the house was originally given a preservative coat of limewash, making it not a red hall, but a white hall.

Numbers 15 and 16 Mardol and Number 1 Hills Lane. The original 1965 caption for this says 'The owners oppose the council's plan for a preservation order on them.' Was nothing sacred in the sixties? Happily the buildings have survived and today house a splendid gift shop.

The final section of the concrete 1951 Castle Bridge is eased into place, watched by an admiring crowd. The structure replaced an earlier bridge linking Castlefields and Monkmoor just up from the weir. And before that a ferry would transport folk between the two suburbs. The new 237ft bridge was the first of its kind in the country to be built with pre-stressed and tensioned reinforced concrete.

Shrewsbury Technical College in March 1938, the year of its opening. The adjoining black and white building, which dated from 1601, was at this time Merival Garage. The garage signs have been deliberately painted out on this print, probably because of contemporary newspaper sensitivity about giving free advertising. A new edge-of-town technical college opened in 1960 and the old college building became the Wakeman School in 1965. Merival was demolished in 1969.

Wyle Cop School photographed in October 1967.

The former Trouncer's Brewery in Longden Coleham in March 1971. Rowlands & Co fruit merchants had taken over the site about 18 years previously. This picture was taken to record the lowering in height of the chimney stack on the left, which was reduced to 35ft because it was unsafe.

Headquarters of the old Southams' Brewery at Chester Street, pictured in 1966.

It's 1958 and a gentleman on a leisurely walk along the riverside stops to admire the mighty bridge which supports Shrewsbury railway station. These days the bridge no longer has a covered roof. Completed in 1848, the town's magnificent station boasts a fine frontage in Tudor-gothic style. Unbelievably there was, in the early 1970s, a plan to replace it with a modern building, but thankfully the idea was not supported. Thus, while other splendid Victorian stations across the country succumbed to the bulldozers, Shrewsbury's survived. Saints be praised!

The old disused railway workers' canteen building in Scott Street at the Back of the sheds back in 1977. When the locomotive sheds were swept away, there seemed no future for the abandoned canteen. But suddenly its renaissance was being discussed. The Queen's Silver Jubilee celebrations had breathed new life into communities. Residents of Reabrook – invigorated by the way in which the jubilee had brought them together – now wanted a sports and social club. Mr John Archer of Leamore Crescent was voted chairman of a new steering committee and ideas for renovating the old canteen were being looked at. Before long, the people of Reabrook had their sports and social club.

A new view of Shrewsbury Castle was opened up thanks to a big clearance scheme in Chester Street in the 1950s, seen here well under way on 18 February 1957.

Meadow Place car park in Shrewsbury on 15 February 1963, the day before its closure to make way for further redevelopment of the smithfield site. It was said to be one of the town's oldest car parks.

The Raven Meadows multi-storey car park takes shape on 3 April 1968. It was one of the developments on the smithfield site.

A quick glance and you could be forgiven for thinking this is Porthill Bridge. But it is in fact the old Castle Suspension Bridge above the weir at Castlefields which was replaced by a concrete bridge in the 1950s. A shame really – as this is far more attractive than its successor.

Through an archway in Shrewsbury Castle, an observer takes in the view of Castle Street washed in summer sunshine in July 1954.

John Plimmer, the custodian at Shrewsbury Castle, chats with a visitor in February 1953. He had been custodian for so many years that he was regarded as an authority on the castle's history.

A bird's-eye view of the Royal Shrewsbury Hospital complex under construction in the early 1970s.

Work in progress at the Priory Boys School playing fields in 1969.

Sundorne Castle in 1953. The building was already empty and deteriorating when this picture was taken. It was finally demolished in 1955. It had been more of a grand country estate than a castle, and boasted an ornamental lake and extensive grounds. One or two of the smaller buildings escaped demolition.

Shropshire escaped dishonourable mention in a shock report on the state of Britain's public lavatories, said the report accompanying this picture in 1965. 'But it is not free from the attention of the vandals,' it went on. These urinals were to be found under the arches of Shrewsbury's historic market hall in The Square.

Relatively few people know that only 70 steps divide the hustle and bustle of Shrewsbury's town centre streets from the quiet and serenity of the waters of the River Severn. These steps lead from Pride Hill down to Raven Meadows from where it is but a short walk to the river. The picture was taken in 1974. Today the 70 steps – an ancient route – has been incorporated into the development of modern shopping centres.

Even experts on Shrewsbury might be stopped in their tracks by this extraordinary shot. The white building seen at the end of the road on the left is the big giveaway. It is of course The Shrewsbury Hotel, formerly The Britannia Hotel. This, therefore, is Smithfield Road and all the buildings on the right have long since disappeared. This was how it looked in 1938.

Peering up into the middle of this view are the upper storeys of Rowley's Mansion, which means we are in Barker Street. In the foreground is the yard of the New Ship Inn, an old pub cleared away in the massive slum clearances of the 1930s.

Hill's Lane as pictured on a postcard which was franked 13 March 1933.

The end of an era. Massive slum clearance in the 1930s around the Barker Street area.

In 1954 an 8ft wide footpath was cut beside the River Severn in The Quarry. A workman carves out the path on or about 1 June.

A Georgian gem: Beautiful St Chad's Church framed here by the trees in The Quarry park in the 1960s.

Small shops housed within a pretty collection of half-timbered buildings in Abbey Foregate. This was 1972. The businesses may have since changed hands, but the scene today is happily very much the same as it was then.

The Factory Bridge, St Michael's Street, Shrewsbury, in 1954, when this section of the Shrewsbury Canal had been drained and was being filled in. The bridge had been rebuilt in 1913 and the plaque recording this event has been preserved and is now fixed to a wall on the site of the demolished bridge. In the background can be seen the roof of the Ditherington Flax Mill (see next picture).

This is one of the most important buildings in Shrewsbury. As the oldest iron-framed building in the world, it is in fact the great-grand-daddy of New York's skyscrapers. The old Maltings at Ditherington started out in life as a flax mill and indeed is today once again known as Shrewsbury Flaxmill. It is pictured here in March 1960. Today it awaits a multi-million pound renovation as offices, shops, apartments and leisure facilities.

It's spring 1953, and the blossom is out. The picture, dating from around 24 April, was taken from a house in the 'Pig Trough' – a passage in Coton Hill.

Shrewsbury's 'Island of Flowers' – a traffic roundabout at the approaches to the Welsh Bridge – photographed in (we think) the late 1940s. Notice the Anchor Inn advert on the roof of the pub across the bridge and to your right in Frankwell. Note also the Great Western Railway and London Midland and Scottish Railway sign pointing to the station. The railways were nationalised in 1948. The traffic island has long since disappeared.

The Theatre Royal in 1949. In its later days it was the County Theatre cinema, but was severely damaged by fire in 1945. The three figures in the frontage are of Shakespeare, flanked by Comedy and Tragedy. During work in 1953 to convert the premises into Astons furniture store, foreman bricklayer Ted Jacks saved Shakespeare from being carted off to the tip and gave him to his father, Harry, who painted the statue in bright colours and kept it just inside his gateway in Mytton Oak Road. When Harry died Ted inherited the statue, and for years kept it in his garden near Shrewsbury as a sort of glorified garden gnome.

Abandoned and vandalised prefabs in New Park Close, Castlefields, in the summer of 1968, shortly before demolition.

Part of The Meadows estate at Harlescott pictured in 1956.

A row of houses in New Park Terrace, Castlefields, which had, by 1972, been scheduled for demolition. Although some Castlefields houses of this vintage did indeed become victims of the bulldozer at this time, many Victorian streets here have remained untouched. Castlefields is still one of Shrewsbury's most fascinating suburbs and has its very own church in the shape of the lovely All Saints in North Street.

Helicopters from Tern Hill fly in formation over the River Severn and Shrewsbury town centre in 1968.

A rare picture of the locomotive sheds in the days of steam. The complex eventually became redundant and was swept away in the late 1970s. Nevertheless, the neighbouring area of Rocke Street, Rea Street, Scott Street and so on, is still known affectionately as 'the back of the sheds'.

Cold Bath Court in January 1953. It is said that monks used to parade here to take their daily baths.

Nothing much to give the date away here. Indeed, the photograph might almost have been taken yesterday. This is The Gateway House which dates back to 1502. The Lord Marches of Wales annually came from Ludlow to hold their court in the building. Early in the Civil War it was even the home of King Charles I for a while. But this picture was taken a few centuries later in August 1962!

Sir Offley Wakeman, chairman of the Shrewsbury School governors, stands at the microphone making the presentation of the High Cross to the town and corporation of Shrewsbury on 19 June 1952. The cross was given to the town by the school to mark the school's fourth centenary and the goodwill existing between the school and the town. It was received by the Mayor, Alderman Colonel J.M. West, himself a master at the school. In the foreground are the headmaster, Mr J.M. Peterson, and masters; to the left of the cross are the vicar of St Mary's Church, the Revd R.M.B. Mackenzie, and the town clerk, Mr S.R.H. Loxton; to the right of the cross is the Mayor; and behind it are aldermen and councillors.

August 1965 and Mr and Mrs Curtis are outside their leaning home at Town Walls. The scaffolding was in place while workmen gave the stone a facelift.

The October 1970 caption for this picture reads: 'Shrewsbury Town Council's highways committee has been told that an oak tree at Ludford Drive, Mount Pleasant, is dangerous. The tree is to be inspected by a Ministry of Housing Inspector.'

Lit up against the night sky is Shrewsbury Library, once the home of Shrewsbury School. The picture may date from the late 1930s.

A centre of controversy in 1965 (a time when, it seems, nothing was safe from the dreaded bulldozers), this is number 25 High Street, proudly displaying its 1709 date-plate in the centre of the brickwork. 'Should it stay or should it go?' ran the original caption. It seems the firm of Maddox and Company wanted to replace it with another building – which Shrewsbury Corporation maintained would be out of keeping with the buildings on each side. Good on yer, Shrewsbury Corporation. But, on the other hand, isn't this the same Shrewsbury Corporation which just five years later was knocking down the grand Shirehall just a few yards away in The Square? Anyway, the corporation made a preservation order on number 25 and (even though Maddox's appealed to the Minister of Housing and Local Government) the building survived.

Workmen were doing repairs at the Porthill suspension bridge over the River Severn around February 1952. One of the 'hanging rods' had fractured and people walking over the bridge were asked to do so slowly and in single file to avoid it swaying.

The Moat at Harlescott Grange, seen here in about 1972, was being earmarked as a potential ancient monument for the town. But the Mayor of Shrewsbury, Alderman George Farr, thought it was all 10 years too late as the area had already been almost destroyed by children.

Harlescott Grange, the farmhouse which gave its name to a council housing estate, seen on 31 March 1959. There was talk about turning it into a pub to act as the estate's local. In the event the house was demolished and a new pub, called the Anchor, was built from scratch on the site, opening in November 1962.

The Shoemakers' Arbour, which was moved from Kingsland and across the river into The Dingle in 1879, is admired by a man who has since followed the Shoemakers' Guild into history. The year is 1938 and Mr Fred Evans, a Shrewsbury journalist, aged 68, studies the picturesque stonework.

A scene which hasn't changed a bit since this photograph was taken in 1962. The back of Charles Darwin's statue dominates the picture, taken from the archway into Shrewsbury Library. The black and white building is Castle Gates House on the approach to Shrewsbury Castle.

Check out the curvy 1950s cars in the busy car park of the attested dairy section of the cattle market at Harlescott. The main move of the smithfield from the town centre to Harlescott was not until 1959, but the attested dairy section had been at the new site since 1956. This photograph dates from January 1957.

Some of Abbey Foregate's lost cottages. From left are numbers 77, 78, 79, 80 and 81, seen here in 1940. The woman standing in the doorway of number 78 is a woman known as Granny Beddoes. The tree on the right was chopped down in 1948. Nor did the homes themselves survive – they were later demolished.

The Old School House – the former Sundorne School – looks a sorry sight in September 1970. A former teacher at the school, Miss Isabel Robinson, lived in part of the building with her cat Booboo, but died in 1967. It must have been demolished soon after this picture was taken as in 1971 Gordon Croxton saw the work going on and bought two lorryloads of the dressed stone – the rubble of the old school – to build a wall to replace a hedge at his home in Wellington Road, Muxton.

The water tower at Shelton nears completion in January 1935. It meant that Shrewsbury residents would soon get drinking water in their homes, rather than water having to be drawn from conduits in the town streets.

Shrewsbury Technical College students study the first phase of work on Shrewsbury's new swimming pool in November 1967.

At the time, a badly neglected old lady of the townscape, this is Howard Street Warehouse, once the terminal warehouse for part of the Shropshire Union Canal and by the early 1970s, threatened with extinction. Shrewsbury Town Council's highways and planning committee had agreed (in 1973) to British Rail's request that the listed building should be demolished. Its fate rested with the Department of the Environment. Thank goodness common sense won the day and the structure was later fully renovated as The Buttermarket nightclub and home to the highly respected Shrewsbury Jazz and Roots Club.

Only the cars parked outside give us a clue as to the date of this picture of Darwin House, birthplace of the world famous naturalist, Charles Darwin. The original caption tells us it is in fact October 1969.

The famous Palin's Cake Shop on the junction of Castle Street and School Gardens in 1914. In more recent times this was Halford's bicycle shop before the firm moved to Meole Brace Retail Park. It was from this legendary emporium (from 1760 onwards) that Mr Palin – 'the prince of cake compounders' – created the county town's much sought after delicacy, the Shrewsbury Cake. Thomas Plimmer later took over the business, turning the premises into a restaurant, but still selling the famous cake.

Meadow Place in January 1934, looking up towards Castle Gates. This can only be demolition work being carried out prior to the construction of the Granada cinema. But it all must have happened very quickly because the cinema actually opened in 1934 – that same year.

No 19 Mardol as it was in 1953 when it was owned by Macfisheries, a national firm of fishmongers who subsequently demolished it in order to modernise their premises. Not long afterwards, the firm moved to another site in the town, and eventually ceased trading. The frontage to Mardol was jettied and the whole concept was that of a shop or shops at ground level with the owner's prestigious accommodation above. Opinions vary on how great a loss it was to Shrewsbury's heritage when this building was demolished, but fortunately a similar block remains further down Mardol, much disguised, and incorporating Nos 12, 13 and 14.

A fascinating little picture of the old mint at Shrewsbury, a shot used on a postcard in the 1930s. Parts of the ancient mint are now cleverly incorporated into the modern-day fabric of shops on Pride Hill.

Looking at those cars this could almost be a scene from a Laurel and Hardy film. Of course it's the English Bridge which links the town centre to Abbey Foregate. And although the caption on the postcard says 'New English Bridge, opened August 1927' the grand old bridge is really much older than this and was merely widened in the 1920s to cope with the demands of increasing volumes of traffic. On the extreme left can be glimpsed the old technical college which was later replaced by The Wakeman School.

Water, Water...

In the year 2000 the waters of the River Severn rose to cause havoc in the county town on a scale not known for half a century. The event will be remembered as the great millennium flood.

First came a storm which ripped across the Shropshire landscape. With rain, lashings of it. Hard on its heels came the rising waters. Higher and higher. The River Severn could not take any more and spilled over vast tracts of countryside as well as hitting places like the Ironbridge Gorge, Bridgnorth and of course Shrewsbury very hard.

Once again, old riverside suburbs like Frankwell and Coleham took most of the punishment. But for such areas, this was nothing new. While the great millennium flood has been well documented elsewhere, in this book we continue to focus our attention further back in time.

The pictures here vividly illustrate that there is nothing new under the sun (or the rain). Meanwhile, debates continue to rumble on about how best to defend the county town from future floods!

A safe crossing for Yvonne Smith, of The Mount, in flooded Frankwell on 15 January 1968. Shrewsbury Corporation employee Eddie 'Butty' Pugh does his good deed for the day. Butty seems to have been quite a man of the floods as he crops up in several of our pictures.

The Floating Restaurant near the Welsh Bridge has not always lived up to its name. But it managed to ride out the storms on 17 January 1974.

A most unusual shot showing the swollen River Severn surging past Coton Hill (with Benbow House on the far left, clearly under water). The picture was taken from the roof of Telephone House in December 1965.

Again December 1965 and Shrewsbury Council workmen prepare for a long, cold and wet vigil during the floods. Somehow they still managed to raise a few smiles as they took a snack on two of the boats brought in for the emergency deliveries.

Just a shower? A nasty downpour in the seventies transforms the scene outside the Exchange Hotel.

The far from gay Gay Meadow is waterlogged in January 1968. It wouldn't be the last time!

And here it is again.

Shrewsbury in flood – just for a change!

One to remember. Crowds watch in awe from the Welsh Bridge during the 1946 flood which was the worst since 1795. Military amphibious vehicles called 'ducks' were used to rescue people and take supplies to countryside areas, while in the county town itself 600 houses were hit. A particular feature was how rapidly the River Severn rose – 4ft in 12 hours on 8 February. Despite the big floods of 2000, the 1946 floods remain the most severe in living memory.

It isn't just the River Severn that misbehaves. The Rea Brook at Meole Brace was a swirling torrent on 25 February 1969, and the banks were crumbling. Parents at nearby homes were calling for safety measures to protect their children.

Mr Alfie Dodwell and his dog are rescued in September 1957 at Frank-well Quay. At the back of the punt is Albert Jones, who worked for Shrewsbury and Atcham Borough Council, while at the bow is Butty Pugh. They are in front of Miss Wainwright's shop, and Miss Flo Wainwright is peeking out of the upstairs window. Looking out of the window a little further along are Mrs Ebrie or Ebury and her daughter Christine.

The 1923 floods in Frankwell. The tall building just left of centre is the Sweep's House, and the nearby garage is Lewis & Froggatt cycle specialists.

Coracle men outside Florrie Wainwright's shop in Frankwell in 1923. Many men in Frankwell still had coracles in those days and a favourite trick to entertain the locals during floods was riding the raging current and shooting under the centre arch of the Welsh Bridge. They had to lie back – there was only just enough room to squeeze under.

Abbey Foregate seriously under water in 1946.

Abbey Foregate seriously under water again – in the 1960s.

It's 1968 and the mop and bucket squads have turned out in Frankwell as clearing up becomes the order of the day. Frankwell has been flooding for centuries so its people are well used to a little water!

Mops and buckets have always had their part to play. This time it's Coleham in December 1964.

Anxious eyes watch the water gauge at the Welsh Bridge as the water rises on 14 December 1964.

Ice floes passing through the town in March 1963. The 1960s saw major changes to the riverside area on the right.

Cars plough through the Frankwell streets on 15 January 1968.

Street Life

Ever popped into town to do a spot of shopping and suddenly noticed that that favourite old shop of yours is no longer there? Well, of course, every year dozens of shops in any town will either move premises or go out of business or else be swallowed up by a larger concern.

That's business. That's life. Blink and you've missed it. That gift shop where you bought your wife a Paddington Bear has vanished without warning. That coffee shop you loved so much? Gone! In fact the subject of 'Shops Of The Past' would make a fascinating book in its own right.

Shrewsbury is a bustling shopping centre and the streets always seem to be thronged with crowds and activity. In this section, then, we celebrate the vitality of the town and bring memories of some old friends you may be missing. Shops like Grocott & Co, Costumiers, who traded in The Square, Preedy's – The Pipe Shop – on Pride Hill, and Mansells Toy Shop on Wyle Cop, to name a few. We also have the bus station in Barker Street. We have St Alkmund's Square before the toilets were built!

There are also evocative images of Castlefields in the early seventies and a host of other treasures. Enjoy!

Castlefields in the 1960s – and specifically that bit of it which was utterly transformed by demolition and modernisation. This is New Park Road. On the left is a small 'Salop Cleaners' and next up is The New Inn. The white-walled pub in the distance is The Bowling Green. Also along this stretch was Stealey's fish and chip shop. Although all this was swept away, much of Victorian Castlefields has survived intact.

To a certain generation this lovely picture of Mansells toy shop on Wyle Cop is powerfully evocative. Like Pickerings in Mardol, Mansells was one of those lovely old-fashioned independent toys shops that existed in an era when Toys'R'Us was not even a twinkle. Look closely and you'll see the once familiar Corgi Toys promotional strip around the tops of the windows. There's also a cowboy hat, dolls, a pedal car and an advert for Bonanza toys. Although the shop (pictured here in 1967) has changed hands several times since, the mosaic doorstep with the word 'Mansells' proudly inset is still there today.

New Park Road again, this time looking in the opposite direction towards the town centre.

One of Castlefields' great survivors – John Street – looking down towards the allotments.

Its fortunes have risen and fallen and risen again as the years have rolled by. This is Mardol, nowadays part of what has become known as Shrewsbury's 'West End'. The area has always been famous for its quirky little shops like Pickering's toy shop which has been known to generations of local children. Here – in this 1964 shot – we can see beyond the Hillman Minx and other cars of the era that The Empire cinema (which opened in 1922 and closed in 1998) is showing Cliff Richard in *Wonderful Life*. This lacklustre musical also starred The Shadows and comedy actors Melvyn Hayes and Richard O'Sullivan as merchant sailors stranded in the Canaries. Oh, yes.

Mardol again, this time in the 1940s, or maybe a little earlier – anyway, pictured on a postcard franked on 4 July 1945. The beautiful half-timbered building on the left is the King's Head pub and the mock-Tudor building in the middle of the picture is The Empire cinema.

Believe it or not, if the original caption to this picture is to be believed, this pedestrian crossing was something of a pioneer for the county town. The photograph was taken on 28 June 1971, and the caption was: 'A new feature of Shrewsbury town streets are pedestrian crossings which have appeared in the last few days. One of the most useful is at the busy crossing point at Barker Street, now in constant use.'

September 1956 and traffic flows over the English Bridge as the River Severn flows beneath it.

The handwritten note on the back of this postcard says 29 June 1941 – but the cars and taxis look earlier than this.

Grocott & Co., costumiers, was one of the big-name shops in Shrewsbury town centre for many years. Those who remember The Square at this time will also doubtless have fond memories of Adnitt and Naughton's, the wonderful old stationers a few doors down.

An early 20th-century view of Frankwell.

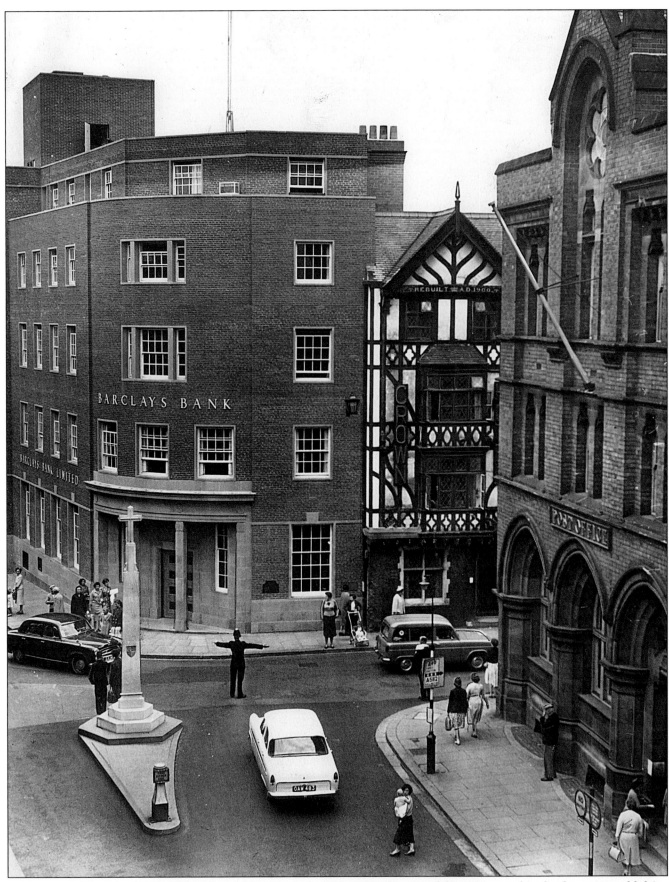

A nice view of the top of Pride Hill in September 1959, before the major changes of the 1960s – and in the days you could drive up Pride Hill, which is now pedestrianised. The post office on the right closed within weeks of this picture and was later demolished and a new post office was built in modern style. The Crown Hotel, despite its Tudor appearance, was in fact built in 1900, and was also demolished not long after this picture was taken. The white Ford Consul was owned, and no doubt being driven at the time, by Mr George Butler of Monkmoor, who bought it in 1957 for £725 and sold it in 1962.

Early 20th-century shot of Butcher Row. The building facing us from the top of the street would eventually be removed and, in the 1950s, modern toilets were built here, backing on to the historic Bear Steps and Fish Street.

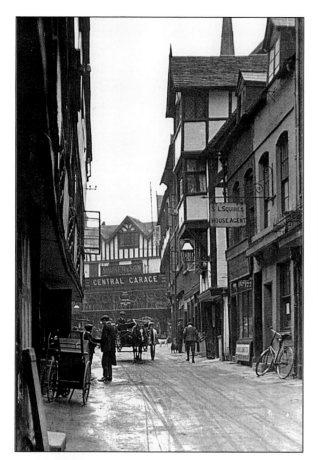

These were the days when it was relatively safe for children to walk down the middle of a street! The picture is taken from a postcard franked 13 July 1929, and shows Wyle Cop free of motor cars.

Wyle Cop again of course – this time in 1964.

A rain-soaked Shrewsbury bus station when it was situated in Barker Street. Among the buses lined up on this day in 1963 were the S11 to Battlefield, the 928 Shawbury service, the 917 to Wellington and the S14 to Moston Road.

Cottages at the corner of Mill Road and Abbey Foregate. The photograph is undated, but is probably in the 1960s. In any event, the cottages had no future – they no longer exist.

A little Austin chugs along Town Walls soon after World War Two. In the background is an Armstrong Siddeley owned by Dr Lawson Stote, which caused something of a sensation. Ordinary folk found it difficult to buy new cars immediately after the war, but doctors could. The late Dr Stote was a well-known Shrewsbury doctor and his daughter Sally thinks the gleaming turquoise car was a Sapphire model. It might be her father standing by the car. The family moved to Swan Hill Court opposite the tower in 1948. But as his surgery was next to the tower, the date could be a little earlier – around 1946 or 1947.

Now this is really going back… This photograph must have been taken before the late 1860s because all the buildings on the right were knocked down then to make way for the Victorian market hall. Among those to meet their doom at the hands of Victorian demolition teams was the King's Arms pub, which is the black and white building in the centre of the row.

An interesting selection of late 1950s and early 1960s cars is on view in this August 1961 picture. Lower Claremont Bank is on the left, together with the approaches to the Welsh Bridge, where a couple of Triumph Heralds are about to pass each other. Close inspection of the bus reveals that the bus conductor (remember bus conductors?) is riding in the doorway. Over the road is Hill's Lane.

In October 1953 Brian Rowe, an 18-year-old apprentice motor mechanic, dressed up as a French Legionnaire and wandered around Pride Hill to promote the film *Desert Legion* starring Alan Ladd at the Empire cinema. He did it as a stunt for the cinema manager Reg Cooper, and it was Reg's wife who created the outfit. The white trousers were a pair of chef's trousers from the restaurant above the Empire and the tunic was, Brian thinks, a GPO coat with some fancy buttons and gold braid added. It did the trick as small boys would ask him: 'Are you on leave from the French Foreign Legion, Mister?' and, according to Brian, the stunt helped swell attendances at the movie.

Eighteen-year-old Jill Allen leans out of the window of what was then Laurents Ladies Hairstylist in medieval Grope Lane on 19 November 1962. Jill lived in Harlescott and was employed by Mrs Helen Brookfield as a junior stylist. She left Shrewsbury in 1963 when the family moved to Jersey, and is now Mrs Jill du Heaume.

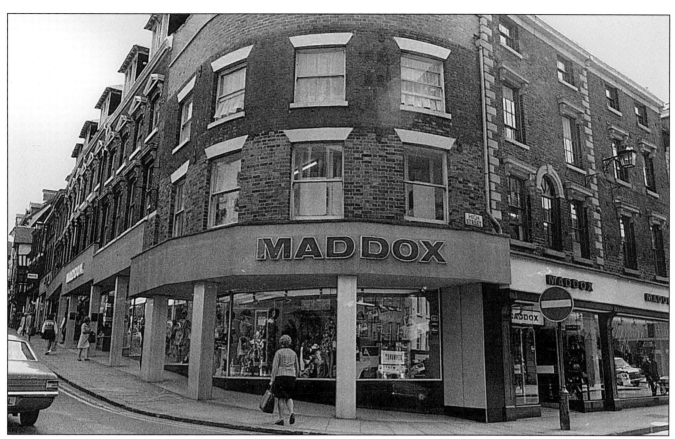

For over 100 years Maddox, at the junction of Pride Hill and High Street, was one of the premier stores in Shropshire. It was opened in 1862 and developed into what was claimed to be the largest department store in the West Midlands. Owen Owen took it over in 1975, shortly after this photo was taken, and it closed in 1990.

Castle Gates – almost unrecognisable from the Castle Gates of today – pictured in the early 1900s. On the right is the Castle Vaults. On the left is the original Station Hotel. The current day Station Hotel is of course further down the road next to Chronicle House and opposite the railway station. The coming of the Granada cinema in the 1930s transformed this scene forever.

Lots of period detail here. The photograph is from November 1959 and the original caption reads: 'Motorists passing over privately-owned Kingsland Bridge in Shrewsbury still have to pay a sixpenny toll.'

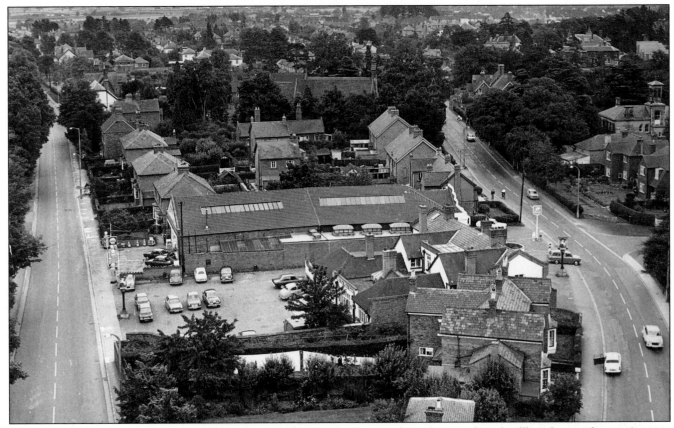

This wonderful bird's-eye view could only have been experienced, of course, from the top of Lord Hill's Column. The year is 1972. The roads (London Road to the left, Wenlock Road to the right) are extraordinarily quiet. Notice how the two petrol stations are in fact one and the same but with forecourts on to both roads. Also note that the houses in the foreground (between the White Horse pub and the Column) have since gone to allow for road widening.

The Exchange Hotel on the corner of Bellstone and St John's Hill captured in around 1935. The Exchange was later demolished and replaced by a more modern pub of the same name.

The old Castle Foregate railway bridge which was due to be reconstructed as this picture was taken in 1962.

Back to The Square and we can see by this time (late sixties) that the once proud Grocott & Co (right) is closed down and up for sale. Also note that the original Shire Hall (left) is still in place, completing a wonderful collection of buildings. Oh, that we could turn back time! The Square is still lovely today, but it has been diminished by the loss of the grand old lady on the left.

St Alkmund's Place in 1968.

Great original caption for this one: 'The demolition of a building has opened up this charming new view in Butcher Row of St Alkmund's Church and churchyard. Last night Shrewsbury Town Council was undecided what to do about the vista. In the end it was decided to take plenty of time to consider the matter before taking a decision.' Apart from the caption using the words 'undecided', 'decided' and 'decision' all in one breath, it is amusing in another way. Because what did the council finally end up doing? Why, of course, they built some toilets here – presumably to further enhance the charming view!

Yet another crane appears on the ever-changing Shrewsbury skyline. Construction work gathers pace (just behind Rowley's House) in the summer of 1962 as the multi-storey car park takes shape.

Still 1962 and as The Beatles begin their march towards world domination a photographer shows the people of Shrewsbury the sort of view they will soon be able to enjoy as the multi-storey car park overlooking Barker Street nears completion. Less than 40 years later the car park would be a redundant eyesore.

Shops and businesses on the Shoplatch side of the old Victorian market hall, probably in the 1950s. From left are the Corn Exchange Billiard Hall, Pet's Corner run by D.H. Twist and J.W. Airey, and, far right, Sheffield's.

Sheffield's was one of the best-known hairdressers in the county town for half a century and during the war it had one very famous customer – Haile Selassie, who was in Shropshire during his enforced exile from Ethiopia.

Bizarre times! It's the 1960s and bulldozers across the nation are having a field day. Against this backdrop a critic says of Frankwell (photographed here in September 1965) that it has 'gone almost too far to be saved'. Well, some of it was torn down, but thankfully much survived, and this scene has not changed so very much since the picture was taken.

Loss and Renewal

The Shire Hall in The Square and the grand Victorian market hall were two of the most imposing buildings in the town. But the prevailing philosophy of the 1960s and early 1970s was that the old needed to be swept aside in favour of the new.

Were there those in the town at the time who spoke out against this demolition? Or was the concept of preservation yet to be invented? We can't help thinking that had these two elaborate structures somehow managed to survive into the 1980s then they would surely still be with us today.

The mood by then had changed. People were beginning to really appreciate the history around them. Ah well.

Let's hope these were among the last big scale demolition jobs within the town centre. A town's architectural heart is not just made up of the magnificent. There is also the mundane. Like the Chanticleer Chinese Restaurant in the Riverside Shopping Centre and the Green Shield Stamp shop in Barker Street.

Memories are made of this!

Time to grab a tissue and shed a tear or two. Some bright sparks had decided the Shire Hall in The Square was past its sell-by date. Okay, beauty may be in the eye of the beholder, but how can Princess House be seen as an improvement? This is one case where a long-term strategy with an eye on heritage and tourism would have come in handy.

The madness of the sixties spills over into the seventies. It is January 1971 and the old Shire Hall is ripped apart. Wouldn't these lovely rooms have made a splendid museum and art gallery?

The emotionless caption of the day reads: 'A new skyline has appeared in Shrewsbury Square as the demolition of the old Shire Hall gets under way. Shops and offices will be built in its place.'

'The Old Shire Hall, on which demolition men have been working for some months, stands forlornly in Shrewsbury Square,' reads the caption of the day. 'But not for long because work is expected to be over soon.'

It's April 1971 and the strangely ancient-looking wrecking equipment has done its job.

Yes, it's an interesting view – but what a loss!

And so to another tale of urban renewal. One of the Column's lions watches over the old Column Lodge which stood in what was to become the forecourt of the new Shirehall at the junction of Abbey Foregate and London Road. The Lodge had to go – and with it the job for an ex-soldier who was the 'Keeper of the Keys' and who allowed visitors access to Lord Hill's Column.

The first aerial view of Shrewsbury's giant new Shirehall – it is normally spelt as one word these days – taken by Bob Craig of the *Shropshire Star* in June 1965.

Shrewsbury's giant Shirehall takes shape in 1966, the shadow of Lord Hill's Column making an appearance in the bright sunshine.

A special day for Shrewsbury as the Queen visits in March 1967 to officially open the Shirehall.

With structures like this, you really need a sense of perspective. Here's an interesting view of the Shirehall with Lord Hill's Column in the background.

A sight to stir the soul, but in all the wrong ways. Telephone House goes up during the winter of 1961 and 1962. In more recent years the building has become something of an embarrassment and is regularly identified in lists of the least attractive modern buildings in the town.

Try turning this one upside down for an unusual view of Telephone House. The car park on the old smithfield site was so wet in 1967 that motorists complained that they had to pay 'mooring fees'.

Shrewsbury didn't seem to care when Merival was demolished in September 1969. No formal protests were received when demolition notices were posted by the county council. Demolition consent was given by the government on the grounds that the 17th-century building was incapable of restoration. The oldest part is on the left, the other parts being later additions which were painted to give a black and white effect.

The beginning of the end for a sizeable chunk of Shrewsbury's 'Little Borough' at Frankwell as an eight-man demolition team prepares to undertake a three-week clearance operation in 1963.

Oakley Manor in Belle Vue undergoing conversion into new offices for Atcham Rural District Council in July 1965.

The statue of Eureka at Shrewsbury's new technical college in September 1960 – the year of its opening.

The demolition of the old county fire service headquarters in Cross Hill approaches completion on 3 November 1976. The building, along with the neighbouring old county police station, was knocked down to make way for 36 new old people's homes.

This is a view of the rear of the one-up, one-down Draper's Almshouses in St Mary's Street on 21 February 1961, which was towards the end of their days. Elderly residents in the houses opposite St Mary's Church had to share two taps in the cobbled communal yard, which was treacherous in the winter. They were told that the buildings would be demolished within two years and that new dwellings would be found for them in Fairford Place, off Longden Coleham. The house with the ground floor window was the caretaker's residence. The gateway to the street was closed off at night by two wrought-iron gates.

A row of terraced homes in Chester Street meets its end on 29 March 1963, revealing a new angle on a block of railway offices which was dubbed a 'white elephant' at the time.

Find a picture of the old Crown Hotel which once stood on this spot in St Mary's Street and ask yourself – is this sixties office block an improvement? At the same time think about Woolworths replacing the Raven Hotel in Castle Street and about Princess House replacing the old Shire Hall in The Square. Were these not three big mistakes for Shrewsbury town centre?

'Eighty-eight-year-old Mr Sid Owen is believed to be the oldest living Freeman of the Borough of Shrewsbury,' reads the original 1974 caption for this picture. 'He was sworn in with three of his six brothers in 1930 – exactly 100 years after his grandfather became a freeman. Now, Mr Owen, of 96 New Park Street, Castlefields, is waiting to move into a new bungalow in nearby Argyll Street. His house is the last one in a terrace.' A touching, human story behind the demolition of New Park Road in the early seventies.

St Mary's Roman Catholic School as it was in its ornate Victorian home, photographed in 1967, before being transferred to a modern building in Castlefields.

Suburbia on the march. The meeting hall (left) and shopping centre at Heath Farm Estate to the north of Shrewsbury. This huge Fletcher estate grew up in the late sixties and early seventies. This shot is from December 1967. The long building on the left is now the home of BBC Radio Shropshire.

Not every 1960s development was bad. The Civic Trust commended this Shrewsbury Corporation scheme, known as Natty Price's Corner, at Frankwell. Note how the entrances of the homes, which are pictured here in April 1963, were built above the flooding level.

The String of Horses stood in Frankwell for almost 400 years before it disappeared to be replaced by, of all things, a traffic island. Happily it was carefully dismantled, and taken to the Avoncroft Museum of Historic Buildings near Bromsgrove in 1971. It was rebuilt, and reopened, in 1976, and the ground floor is now the museum shop. The building dated from 1576 and for much of its history was a coaching inn, going by a number of names. In its last years it was Shrewsbury Co-op shop. These must be its last days in Shrewsbury – the 'Sold' signs are in the window.

The Chanticleer Chinese restaurant was part of the Riverside Shopping Centre. This picture dates from 1969.

Work gets under way on the new swimming pool on 31 May 1967, with the old pool with its distinctive dome in the background. The old pool dated from 1894. The dome was between the two pools, called the Long Plunge and the Short Plunge. Underneath it was the central kiosk.

Sign of the times. The Green Shield Stamps shop which was in Barker Street.

Another modern building makes its mark upon Shrewsbury town centre. Directly opposite beautiful St Mary's Church, these are the offices of the Royal Insurance Group, unveiled in 1966.

And another 'newcomer', Lloyds Bank, which, believe it or not, won an architectural merit award. Whether its design blends in with its near neighbours – Ireland's Mansion on the left of the picture and Owen's Mansion on the right – is perhaps debatable. What do you think?

The Raven Hotel in August 1959. The story which accompanied this picture said: 'Woolworths are interested in buying Shrewsbury's Raven Hotel. This was revealed to the *Express and Star* this morning by Mr A.J.H. Perry, senior member of the family concern owning the Raven Hotel. But Mr Perry emphatically denied rumours that the deal with Woolworths had already been signed and said that a figure of £100,000, which has been mentioned in these rumours, was "absolute nonsense". Considering the fate of the Raven, we now know it couldn't all have been gossip...

Now here is a story to make lovers of Victorian architecture weep. By the bulldozer-crazy 1960s the old market hall (erected 1869) had come to be considered well past its sell-by date. No mercy was to be shown. It had to go. Now okay, maybe by this time it had become run-down and dirty, but just imagine what a gem Shrewsbury would now have if this giant had been cleaned up, renovated and given modern facilities inside. Instead, the old lady was smashed to the ground.

The destruction gets under way. Demolition crews begin their task in 1961. Whatever happened, we wonder, to the magnificent stone coat of arms above the date plate, or to the splendid clock faces on the tower? Could these not have been saved and used as features elsewhere in the town? Was everything destroyed?

The indignity of it all! A once-proud building is pulled to pieces while an uncaring public goes about its business.

The clock tower is all but gone in this 1961 shot from St John's Hill.

A delightful scene, looking down St John's Hill in October 1938. Livesey's, the printers, is on the right. Their name can still be seen in the mosaic of the doorstep, but the company has long since moved on to modern premises on the outskirts of town. The Theatre Royal is the large building on the right – now Poundstretcher. But the vista is once again dominated by the Victorian market hall.

With the first stage of the demolition almost completed, a new attraction appears on the skyline – that of the tower of St Chad's Church.

While construction of the new market carried on at the one end of the complex, shops at the old end continued to trade – despite the sad broken windows of the upper storey. The days of the little roundabout in the foreground were numbered.

In keeping with its surroundings? Hardly! But this was obviously not a major consideration in the sixties.

And there goes the little roundabout in Belmont. It's 1964 and amidst the demolition we can just see the top of a double decker bus (once so familiar in Shrewsbury) peeping over the rubble to the right of the picture.

It's 1965 and the replacement market hall is taking shape. The 200ft high clock tower would soon become a familiar feature on the Shrewsbury skyline. Will townsfolk come to treasure this monster as a period piece – or will it eventually go the same way as its predecessor?

Shoplatch is completely dominated by the market hall complex. The scene has not changed significantly since this 1974 photograph was taken.

Aggggghhhh!!! The monster towers over Shrewsbury's historic streets. Whose idea was this?

The Vibrant Town

Just think for a moment or two about the amazing scope of activities that takes place within a town. Religious events, political events, sporting and recreational activities, the arts, theatre, music… the list goes on.

There are the small things – like shopping or decorating the spare room. There are the big things too, like weddings and funerals. Here, we zoom in on a handful of events, some big, some small.

Royal visits to Shrewsbury are well remembered by her citizens of course. The crowds turned out, the flags were waved, the bunting flapped in the breeze. So where were you on the day Her Majesty came to town? Some of these historic visits are represented in the following pages.

Also here are more everyday events, a wide range of human endeavour from performing in the operatic society to police officers training their dogs, from posting letters of protest to the Government to marching with the Royal British Legion.

It's all part of the tapestry of life in a vibrant town like Shrewsbury.

Shrewsbury turned out in force to welcome the 2nd Battalion of the King's Shropshire Light Infantry 'home' in April 1935. The battalion marched through Shropshire and to Shrewsbury in what was said to be their first official visit for 118 years. The whole town turned out to welcome the troops, who on their arrival were presented with an address of welcome by the Mayor, Mrs M.W. Cock. They stayed a week before going to Hereford to lay up the old colours, and new colours were presented by the Duke of York. The battalion, formerly the 85th Light Infantry, had last visited Shropshire in 1817.

A sea of smiling faces to meet Santa in the 1950s.

A couple of schoolgirls tread carefully as they make their way down the Bear Steps in October 1968.

Lieutenant Colonel N.C. Faithfull, of Marshbrook, brought a wild falcon along to Shrewsbury when he lectured to Shropshire Ornithological Society on falconry. Elizabeth and Henry Wright got a close look. The picture dates from January 1957 or 1958.

Margaret Hill, a 21-year-old beautician, drops a letter into the world famous hexagonal Victorian post box in The Square in April 1972. It was claimed to be one of only two of its kind in the country.

When the Prince of Wales came to Shrewsbury on 21 June 1932, he arrived by plane, which landed at 'Haw Field', Harlescott. The royal visit was to commemorate the 50th anniversary of the move by Shrewsbury School from its old site at Castle Gates. The three men are unidentified, but are possibly police guarding the plane.

And back to the fifties. The Queen's visit to Shrewsbury in October 1952. The castle makes a perfect setting.

The Queen and the Duke of Edinburgh with the chairman of the governors of Shrewsbury School, Sir Offley Wakeman (centre) and (in front) the headmaster of the school, Mr Peterson.

The bunting flaps in the breeze. The cheering crowds line Castle Street. Her Majesty is in town again – but this time it's 1967.

The Queen Mother inspects junior soldiers on 4 November 1969, before a 40-minute tour of the Light Infantry Depot.

Of the hundreds of schoolchildren who lined the route of the Queen Mother's visit to the Sir John Moore Barracks on 24 April 1974, none was more thrilled than four-year-old Richard Jones. Richard was one of the youngest pupils of Woodfield County Infants School and was asked by the Queen Mother if he would like to become a soldier. With a polite touch of his cap he said: 'I haven't decided, Ma'am.'

Christina Corn, 20, from Shrewsbury, admires a suit of armour during a visit to Rowley's House in July 1961. The armour had never seen a battlefield, but had been worn as recently as the mid-19th century by the Vulcan Guilds of Shrewsbury at the annual Shrewsbury Show.

Bill Thacker takes a close look at some of the town's civic plate in April 1955. The items were about to go on show for the King's Shropshire Light Infantry bicentenary. The large piece, in the centre, was presented by the merchants of Kingston, Jamaica, in 1823. Mr Thacker was the mayor's secretary for 28 years.

A Brownie at last, as Sonia Chambers holds the Brown Owl, at enrolment night at the Springfield Brownies in May 1969. Eight girls were finally made Brownies after months of waiting. With Sonia are, left, kneeling, Christine Nichols, Julie Schorah, Nicola Osbourne and Karen Dooglan with back, from left, Susan Jones, Tina Sandford, and Teresa Morris.

A gipsy camp in Sutton Lane in March 1966.

IN MEMORY OF SAMUEL GEORGE LAKE 1871 - 1944 A PIONEER OF THE LABOUR MOVEMENT IN SHREWSBURY

The Rt Hon P.J. Noel-Baker, Secretary of State for Air, unveils a plaque to a Shrewsbury Labour Party pioneer, Samuel George Lake, at the Morris Hall in March 1947, as Mr Lake's widow looks on.

Officials of Shrewsbury Labour Party at the Morris Hall on 9 July 1967, with Richard Crossman, the Leader of the House of Commons (centre), who was the chief speaker at a Labour conference.

There are some funny people about in Shrewsbury! Members of Shrewsbury Amateur Dramatic Society prepare for their latest presentation in February 1968.

A queue of football enthusiasts at the Gay Meadow on Sunday 27 February 1966. They were after tickets for Shrewsbury Town's FA Cup fifth-round game against Chelsea at Stamford Bridge. Tickets were limited, and many returned home disappointed.

Paws for thought. Shrewsbury Police present a dogs' demonstration in 1968.

A moment of quiet prayer in the recently remodelled chapel of St Winefride's Convent of Mercy at College Court on 11 July 1968. The convent celebrated its centenary on 16 July that year.

Sister Agnes, left, and Sister Borgia enjoy a game with pupils of St Winefride's in July 1968.

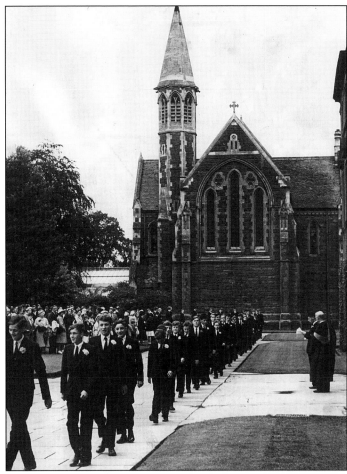

Shrewsbury School speech day in June 1958. It began with the traditional calling-over by the head of the school, A.T. Macaulay. The boys file past and acknowledge their names.

A petition signed by over 1,000 ratepayers supporting so-called 'dirty jobs' strikers in Shrewsbury was handed over to the Mayor of Shrewsbury, Councillor Vic Pierce, on 26 November 1970. Members of the deputation, from left, were: Mr Douglas Purcell, Mr R. Tilke, Mr F. Morris, Mr H. Fellows, and Mr Paul Beard.

A women's meeting – possibly of Women's Institutes – in the Music Hall in the 1950s. Look closely though and you will spot a couple of men on the second row.

Back in 1970 everybody was talking about 'high speed gas'. But it was a bit of a bad joke for Mrs Phyllis Wareham, of Beeches Lane, Town Walls. She waited 14 months to get the water heater in the bathroom of her terraced home repaired.

Brownies, guides and rangers of the 16th Shrewsbury Company held a concert in St George's Hall in March 1969 to raise money for their summer camp and to attain their badge for entertainment. One of the items in the concert was a folk song group led by guide and ranger leader Gill Mulroy (seated).

A bring and buy sale followed the official opening of Bromley House old people's home at Copthorne by the matron, Miss Elsie Llewellyn, in August 1968.

Students from the Shrewsbury Art College, from left, Penny Corbett, Angela Davies and David Walker, busy on their knitting marathon, scheduled to last a week, in The Square, in June 1963. The students were working in two-hour shifts through the day and night and were aiming to knit long strips suitable to make up into blankets for distribution by the Oxford Fund for Famine Relief.

It's 1974 and Shrewsbury Amateur Operatic Society holds a rehearsal of *Charlie Girl*, their latest production, at Coleham Junior School. From left: Geoff Blower, Margaret Gittins, Brian Perry, Ceclia Perry, Ken Jones, Pauline Paton, Joan Plinning (producer) and Sydney Donnell.

A flare-up at night in the county town – but with a difference. This was one of the many flare-off points as the last of the old gas was burned off to make way during conversion for North Sea gas. The burning gas made an unusual meeting point for youngsters on 18 October 1971.

About £100 was raised by 24 members of Shrewsbury Young Liberals in October 1970 when they took part in a 22-mile sponsored walk from Shrewsbury to Montgomery. It was in aid of the Liberal election fighting fund and Liberal social work.

The civil defence rescue team of Chatwood Safe and Engineering Company at Harlescott in the 1950s. Back, from left: George Fearan or Ferron, Tom Wickstead, Horace Heath, and Alf or Sam Evans. Front: Derek Miles, Ernie Golby, and Bill Wilkes. The company was part of the Hall Engineering group and they were all volunteers who trained one night a week at Hall Engineering.

The opening of Shrewsbury bypass in 1933. The ceremony was performed by the Princess Royal. A huge rise in traffic during the 1920s led to many road improvements in Shropshire. The county's first bypass of all was opened at Gobowen in 1926.

Mrs F.O. Burns, of Shrewsbury, holds a plaque which was presented to the Mayor of Shrewsbury by Major General J.M.L. Grover, Colonel of the regiment, on behalf of the King's Shropshire Light Infantry at regimental bicentenary celebrations in April 1955.

Among the many crosses placed at the foot of the war memorial for the annual service of dedication for Poppy Day at St Mary's churchyard in November 1972 was one from five-year-old Alison Israel-Binding, of Grinshill Drive, Monkmoor. She was helped by Mr Bill Thomas, secretary of the Shrewsbury branch of the Royal British Legion and secretary and treasurer of the Shrewsbury Poppy Day committee.

Democracy in action! Shrewsbury pensioners attempt to make their voices heard at the highest level in September 1971 by posting protest letters to government minister Sir Keith Joseph.

Shropshire branch of the British Red Cross Society held a coffee morning and monthly Little Ernie competition at the Morris Hall. Preparing for the competition back in December 1971 are, from left, Mr J. Albutt, Mrs M. Lumsden, president, Miss M. Meredith, county secretary, Commander C.R. Woodhall, and Mrs M. Brown, organising secretary.

Recreation and Fun

Shrewsbury's beautiful Quarry park photographed in a bygone age… Her Majesty the Queen at the West Mid Show… and Miss Shropshire with her attendants ready to head the procession in the 1953 Shrewsbury Carnival. These are among the evocative images we have for you in this section which takes a look at the (largely) innocent recreation and fun enjoyed in the county town over past decades.

While browsing, see if you can recognise anyone in the queue outside one of the tents at Shrewsbury Flower Show in August 1947. Or wonder at the crowds loving every minute of the 1948 Pengwern Regatta. Ah, yes – simple pleasures. And so terribly, terribly English, don't you think?

Also in this section you'll find some wonderful pictures of Shrewsbury Town Football Club – from action at the Gay Meadow in the 1950s to the club's most famous player, Arthur Rowley, being congratulated by fans after breaking the all-time scoring record with the 411th league goal of his career.

Amazing stuff.

The crowd for *It's A Knockout* on 18 May 1969, when Shrewsbury took on Chester. The popular TV wacky games show was recorded in The Quarry, and then broadcast four days later. Shrewsbury won by 14 points to 5.

The entire Shrewsbury *It's A Knockout* team which beat Chester.

The cheerleaders spur the home team to victory.

Fun and games in The Quarry.

The Mayor of Shrewsbury, Councillor Mrs Gwen Dyas, presents the *It's A Knockout* trophy to Shrewsbury's team manager Stuart Lister.

Actor Sid James signs autographs for members of the Shrewsbury *It's A Knockout* team at the finals in Blackpool in September 1969. Before a television audience estimated at 100 million, Shrewsbury were joint winners with a German team from Wolfsburg. Such was the interest in the county town that pubs reported a dip in trade that night.

Queues form to enjoy the hire boats on the River Severn in the summer of 1957. This is a view from the Kingsland Bridge.

Beautiful tree-lined Quarry Avenue in the town's glorious park – pictured here on a postcard dated 7 August 1924.

'Shrewsbury's Dingle at this season of the year is lovely with cherry blossom,' reads the original caption for this May 1952 photograph by J.E.J. Whitaker of 9 Berwick Road, Shrewsbury.

Tidying up the ornamental pond in The Dingle in 1953.

Miss Shropshire and her attendants assemble at Shrewsbury Castle ready to head the street procession on its way to The Quarry in the 1953 Shrewsbury Carnival. Miss Shropshire was Kathleen Bright of Dorrington and the runners-up for the title flanking her were, left, Primrose Mills of Bayston Hill and right, Maureen Basley of Donnington.

Taff Lewis and Mr R.F. Harrison, both of Shrewsbury, were among the first fishermen to arrive at Shrewsbury weir on the opening day of the salmon season in February 1962.

A queue outside one of the tents at Shrewsbury Flower Show in August 1947.

She's back again. This time the Queen is at the West Mid Show in 1975, greeting the Hereford prizewinners.

A fisherman in a coracle ignores a pair of preening swans on a sunny day near the Welsh Bridge in July 1952.

The original caption for this June 1948 picture was: 'Pengwern Regatta was held at Shrewsbury in warm sunshine on Saturday. Many visitors used their precious standard ration and gave their cars an airing. The man in the foreground, however, preferred a quiet nap on the bank to the rigours of rowing.'

It may not look like it, but this is a water-borne demonstration back in May 1960. It was organised by the Shropshire Boat Users Association, whose members formed an armada of boats which sailed to show how many people used the River Severn for leisure. They appear to have been campaigning for a lock to be built at Shrewsbury weir.

The Short Plunge pool at the old town swimming baths early in the 20th century. At the gable end is the shower area and in the corner is the door for the gents' toilets. The men's changing cubicles are along the wall.

An interesting comparison with the previous picture. Shrewsbury and District Schools' Sports Association's 15th annual swimming gala at Shrewsbury Baths on 1 July 1968. It must have been among the last events held in the baths before they were demolished.

Shrewsbury Town in the early 1920s. Standing, right, is Dr Aubrey Ireland, who had a doctors surgery in the town and was a director of the club.

Action at the Gay Meadow in the 1950s.

Shrewsbury Town's greatest, Arthur Rowley, is congratulated by fans at the Gay Meadow as he comes off at half-time after breaking the all-time British leagues' scoring record with the 411th league goal of his career, against Millwall, on 26 September 1962. He beat the 410 of the previous holder, Jimmy McGrory, of Celtic. He scored with 'one of his finest right foot scoring shots of his career'.

Rowley heads home to break Dixie Dean's aggregate scoring record of 379 in a match at Bradford on 29 April 1961.

Player-manager Rowley addresses players at Shrewsbury Town in the 1960s.

'Mr Goals' leads the team out at the Gay Meadow for his least league game in April 1965.

Work and Play

Tourists are beguiled by the medieval architecture of Shrewsbury. But it has always been a town of trade and industry – even, at one time, a port. And it is too Shropshire's major administrative centre and the transport hub of the county.

Busy, busy, busy. So Shrewsbury folk have always made time to relax too. The hustle and bustle of Shrewsbury market in the 1960s. Young lads fishing at the Weir in Castlefields. And an 18-year-old Judy Usher from Church Stretton working hard amidst the steam at the County Cleaners in Shrewsbury in 1965… These are just some of the snapshots of the past gathered together in this section.

Then we have workers on strike at the Rolls-Royce factory in the 1970s, boys enjoying the Shrewsbury School Regatta, and the Royal Observer Corps working through exercises at their Shrewsbury headquarters. Also here are excited youngsters awaiting the arrival of Santa Claus in 1952, a high-wire act, bee-keeping, bottling at the brewery, and a 'new ward' at Copthorne Hospital complete with giant television set!

One of the more intriguing photographs, though, is a nice shot of a new postbox being installed in 1969 – a visual composition which curiously echoes the famous wartime shot of American troops raising the flag on Iwo Jima. We can only assume this was not something the photographer was conscious of at the time!

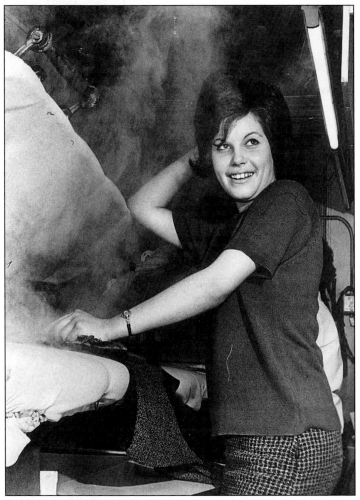

Judy Usher, 18, from Church Stretton, worked at County Cleaners in Shrewsbury as the 'presser' and would literally disappear in a cloud of steam over 200 times a day and still come up smiling. Here she is hard at work on 26 April 1965.

Castle suspension footbridge withstood a five ton test of its efficiency in April 1947. Five trucks loaded with sand crossed the bridge.

Whether the photographer was conscious of it or not, this photograph has echoes of the famous wartime shot of American troops raising the flag on Iwo Jima. In this case though it's the installation of a new postbox which was causing all the effort back in February 1969. The aperture of the old postbox at Bellstone was continually becoming blocked because businessmen in the area were posting large quantities of bulky letters and papers. The solution was to exchange the double-aperture box from Hills Lane for the one at Bellstone.

A huge glass chandelier worth over £1,000 was scrapped by the Granada Theatre because it did not fit in with the redevelopment of the cinema into a bingo club in 1973.

Margaret Lyons, left, and Lesley Owen, were preparing to cast their spell over the guests at a Halloween dance at Yockleton. But first they posed for a photographer in The Quarry on 29 October 1969.

Contrast this hive of activity with the scene that greets you today as you walk into Shrewsbury Market. All was hustle and bustle in 1965.

The racing waters of Shrewsbury's weir have provided an attractive scene for generations. This is September 1955 and the young anglers are Malcolm Sambrook, Don Rogers and Roland Wycherley. Roland would later become a successful businessman and the chairman of Shrewsbury Town Football Club.

Ivan Karle set out to prove his claim that he was the world's smallest strongman at the demolition site of the old Shirehall on 12 January 1971. Ivan, 4ft 10ins and a member of the Robert Brothers circus which was at the Granada in the town at the time, lifted 'Big Bob', a 21 stone, 6ft 6ins demolition worker, 18ins off the ground with his teeth and held him. With the weight of Ivan's two stone lifting table included, the total weight was 23 stone, over twice the strongman's own weight.

Champagne corks popped at the RAF careers office in St Mary's Street to celebrate the 700th recruit to pass through the office, in August 1972. The recruit was Miss Gillian Brown, of Sutton Hill, Telford, who enlisted as a trainee dental hygienist, and was congratulated by Squadron Leader E. Wynn-Davies and Warrant Officer J.B. Jones, the recruiting officer.

This gateway has seen some history. The Sentinel Works on Whitchurch Road, Shrewsbury, originally produced highly-successful steam wagons. The factory was later taken over by Rolls-Royce. Here, in 1971, it is the scene of strike action. Pickets on duty outside the main entrance to Rolls-Royce talk to two employees reporting for work. Another 200 workers at the factory were set to lose their jobs following earlier redundancies.

Shrewsbury's dustmen were issued with new overalls in summer 1969 and transformed into what were claimed to be among the best-dressed refuse collectors in the country. The borough council had hired the overalls from a laundry in the town after complaints from the dustmen that people had said they looked like tramps. The men were paying 1s 3d a week towards the 4s it cost to rent the overalls, including cleaning and replacement. The picture shows Mr D.H. Perry at work.

October 1971 and for the Rolls-Royce workers an almost unanimous vote declares: 'Everybody back!'

Shrewsbury School had its annual procession of boats on the River Severn in the summer of 1954 – and the crowds loved it.

A crowd of children and their parents wait at The Quarry in eager anticipation of the arrival of Santa around 1952.

The Shrewsbury School Regatta – this time in 1968.

The crowd at Shrewsbury Flower Show in the 1920s. They may be looking at the high wire act. Note the stage in the background.

The Marchitas, the 'cyclo-antics' from Germany, entertain the crowd at the 1964 event.

At the 1959 show Jane Faithfull of Church Stretton volunteered to try the high wire. She crossed the wire 70ft above the ground on the back of the high wire artiste.

142

A small crowd gathered round Peter Allwood to see his beekeeping demonstration at the 1964 show.

The date of this picture is unknown but it is most certainly pre-1959 when the livestock market moved to Harlescott.

The livestock market with the Albert Hotel (the white building) clearly in the background. This is probably the late-1950s.

An industrial dispute involving Shropshire firefighters in December 1977. 'Ask pickets outside Shrewsbury Fire Station how they will cope this Christmas,' says the original caption. 'They will tell you – How would you cope on nothing?'

July 1970 and 23-year-old Savitri Sookoo, a trainee nurse at the Royal Salop Infirmary, gives us a warm smile. Says the caption: 'She arrived in Shrewsbury seven months ago from her home in San Fernando, Trinidad, to start a seven month course to become a State Registered Nurse. The clinical teacher at the training school, Miss J.M.P. Powell, watches her at work.'

A captive audience. Mail bag sewing at Shrewsbury prison in 1964.

Hard at work in the assembly shop of a Shrewsbury factory in 1965. These are employees of Hartley Electromotives Ltd.

The 'Lollipop Man' at the children's crossing on St Michael's Street in May 1967 was retired hairdresser Mr Frederick Ridley. He had been helping the children across since the previous August.

Shrewsbury firemen clad in the protective kit necessary when dealing with some forms of chemical tanker accidents. The men here are using special breathing apparatus in February 1965.

February 1963 and the aftermath of the big freeze-up when extreme winter temperatures had played havoc with services. Here, a team of Gas Board service workers prepare to drill into a fractured main at Harlescott in their day and night battle which has gone on for the last six weeks, repairing and relaying new services to consumers. Works maintenance chargehand Mr Cyril Jones, wearing a trilby, said this was the worst situation he had known in almost 40 years with the West Midland Gas Board.

Preparing for Armageddon! To mark the opening of the recruitment drive by the Shrewsbury Royal Observer Corps, the Mayor of Shrewsbury, Councillor Sidney Osborne, visited the head-quarters in May 1963. He is pictured in the plotting room, with Leading Woman Observer Elizabeth Mallett (left) and Woman Observer Francis Munro. Shrewsbury Observer Commander Mr P. Barber is on the extreme right.

A scene of quiet concentration in the headquarters of the Royal Observer Corps in Shrewsbury, the nerve centre of the West Midlands Nuclear Warning and Monitoring Organisation. The HQ was in Holywell Street, Cherry Orchard. The building still exists, albeit with a less apocalyptic role nowadays. These members were a small section of the 600 men and women who formed the Number 16 Group of the ROC which was described as the 'trigger' of the Royal Air Force V Bomber Force and the fall-out 'eyes' of the nation in the event of a nuclear war.

From nuclear war to ladies' undergarments. This is the Silhouette factory at Harlescott photographed in 1970. The building was later taken over by British Telecom. In the background you can spot the old signal box which stands next to the level crossing where the Shrewsbury-Crewe line intersects Harlescott Lane. The signal box, still in use today, was built by the London and North Western Railway in the 1850s.

The swimwear production lines at the Harlescott Lane factory of Silhouette in the seventies.

Bottling at Trouncer's Brewery, Longden Coleham, in 1921. Left is Mrs Ellen Kelly, known as Nell, working with Miss Gladys Horton. The procedure for dealing with broken bottles was simple – they were thrown through the window on the right into the River Severn.

A new ward at Copthorne Hospital in January 1965. This is the lounge, which was 'fitted with a giant television, one of the most modern of its kind in the county.'

Something very hazardous is going on at the top of Lord Hill's column back on 17 May 1954. At first sight it looks as if it may be one of the periodic brush-ups for Lord Hill's statue, but on closer inspection the man on the ladder appears to be carrying a camera. If so, it's a terrifying way to get a picture over the Shrewsbury rooftops.

Carry on smiling! Shrewsbury Rolls-Royce workers look happy enough in this 1973 shot.

The Quarry covered in snow can be stunningly beautiful, but these chaps have more on their mind than enjoying the scenery. They are busy clearing paths around the Porthill Bridge in February 1966.

Hotels, Pubs, Cinemas…

Shrewsbury has never been short of things to do and places to stay. Through the ages it's been a veritable entertainments and leisure capital. Times change, theatres and cinemas come and go, pubs close, hotels get knocked down.

Shrewsbury continues to have a thriving nightlife and remains a popular place to stay. But turn back the clock 40 years or more and there was a quite different scene. Remember the old Crown Hotel? Well, here it is in all its glory. A black and white beauty that is sadly no longer with us. The White Hart Inn in Mardol? Here it is. The wonderful Raven Hotel on Castle Street? Look no further. And The George Hotel on the corner of Shoplatch? Bulldozed and replaced in the sixties by the first Tesco supermarket in town. But at least we have a picture to remind us of The George.

The Red Barn, the Lion Hotel, the Dun Cow and The Loggerheads are also featured in these pages. Here too are the Century and Empire cinemas,

fondly remembered – along with the magnificent Granada on Castle Gates – by a generation who can recall the golden age of the cinema. The Century gave in to economic pressures in the sixties and became a bingo hall (like so many others around the country). The once mighty Granada, which played host to many of the top names of the day, followed the same path to 'bingo heaven', but, unlike The Century, is still operating today. And the lovely old Empire in Mardol, which opened on Saturday 25 November 1922, bravely carried on as a picture house against all the odds until January 1998. It had just about held on against competition from the big new multiplex at Telford. But the arrival of the multi-million pound eight-screen Cineworld at Old Potts Way in Shrewsbury would finish it off as a commercial concern. Happily the familiar façade of The Empire has now been saved and incorporated into a new development.

Laura The Parrot, seen here around 1952, was one of the features of the Red Barn pub in Longden Road. Laura is being handled by Sammy Brooke, who was landlord of the pub for 57 years. Laura could recite Half a Pound of Tuppenny Rice and would, it is said, call 'Time' at the bar. She – or maybe he, as there is no certainty of the parrot's sex – was kept in the cage on the right. On the left is Sammy's grandson, Colin, and leaning against the bar is Len Jones. Laura died in the late 1960s.

Flip back a few pages to the picture of Crown House in St Mary's Street and compare and contrast. Which bright, enthusiastic planners decided to sweep away the Crown Hotel in favour of a nondescript office block?

In August 1953, coronation year, the lion at the Lion Hotel in Wyle Cop was given a magnificent new coat of gold leaf. The lion had been painted in various shades of cream or stone in the past. The workman is believed to be William Braddock, who at one time was a decorator working for Edwin Coles on the end of Dogpole, but at the time of the picture is thought to have been working for a local firm called Greenwood.

For generations Shrewsbury folk have enjoyed a quiet pint in The Anchor in Frankwell, and for generations the waters of the River Severn have occasionally risen to engulf it. Here it is once again cut off by rising floodwaters in December 1964. Food, milk and other supplies were brought by boat at regular intervals by Nevill Tipton and 'Butty' Pugh. The pub, with a host of other Frankwell businesses, would be badly hit by flooding again in the year 2000.

A fine view from the top of the giant 185ft tower crane erected in Smithfield Road to build Telephone House. Notice the long since gone Victoria Hotel in the centre of the picture. Interestingly, the Birch & Son premises (the white building on the left) has hardly changed at all in all these years. And of course the Proud Salopian (behind the Victoria Hotel) still stands proud today.

The Lion Hotel in June 1935. On the left, projecting slightly into the street, is the room where Charles Dickens stayed in 1838.

All is revealed at the Dun Cow Inn on Abbey Foregate as the original timbers become visible with the removal of rendering in March 1960. The original beams had been covered for 60 years and the work was part of a restoration which saw the replacement of sections of timbers eaten up by death watch beetle.

The Loggerheads in Church Street makes its contribution to Shrewsbury's 'town of flowers' reputation in the summer of 1950.

The White Hart Inn, Mardol, pictured in 1970.

A mural showing two abbots enjoying a jar of ale adds a touch of colour to the Abbots Lounge of Shrewsbury's Monkmoor Hotel. It was painted for the then landlord, Eddie Sykes (right) by a Mr Robson. The photograph dates from 1967.

The Radbrook Hall Hotel, Shrewsbury, in July 1962.

The side of the lovely St Mary's Church to the right. The Yorkshire House pub to the left. The old Nurses' Home at the end of the street. The picture was taken in 1969. Incidentally, the mysterious old Yorkshire House is first recorded as a pub in 1828 and yet an iron back-plate in the fireplace is dated 1679. It was once a coach-house on the Withington run with the 'Withington Carrier' setting off from here.

The Shrewsbury Column Hotel pictured in 1967 before a new road layout put paid to the building.

Much-missed, much-talked about, The Raven Hotel in Castle Street pictured here in the 1950s. Incredibly, it was bulldozed to make way for Woolworths.

Okay, possibly not as fine-featured as The Raven at the other end of town, but The George Hotel also had merit and it too was demolished. In its place came one of Shrewsbury's earliest supermarkets – Tesco – and it was a relatively modest affair compared to today's giant out-of-town superstores. Tesco vacated the site in favour of a huge new store at Harlescott.

Work nears completion at the new Granada Theatre at Castle Gates. The theatre and cinema opened in 1934.

A scale model of a Hurricane fighter is hauled onto the cinema frontage in March 1970. Warrant Officer Ben Jones of the RAF careers office in the town had struck on the idea of arranging a special ceremony at the cinema, to coincide with the showing of the film Battle of Britain, in memory of Shropshire Battle of Britain ace Eric Lock. The fibreglass Hurricane was loaned by RAF Hendon as an added attraction.

Rectifiers and projection equipment is lifted out of the Granada in 1973, the year the cinema turned to bingo.

The first bingo session at the Granada in April 1973. It was officially opened when comedian Dick 'Ooo, you are awful' Emery dropped in.

It is the era of Charlie Chaplin and the silent movies and this is The King's Hall Cinema at the bottom of Wyle Cop, photographed in the roaring twenties. The picture house was later renamed The Century and then went the way of so many others across the country to become a bingo hall. Finally, it was given over to retail use.

Another shot of the same building, this time in its Century incarnation in 1962. Town Walls, to the right, runs up to the Roman Catholic Cathedral and The Quarry beyond. The back of Bowens carpet and furniture store is on the right. Quite what happened to the Century's clock is something of a mystery. Unlike the King's Hall's original elaborate entrance, the clock clearly survived the sixties make-over, but then vanished in the 1980s.

Signs of the times. Anthony Booth, later to become father-in-law to Prime Minister Tony Blair, is one of the comedy actors billed here outside The Empire cinema in Mardol as starring in the sex comedy *Confessions of a Driving Instructor*. Robin Askwith was the main star, of course, appearing in a whole series of 'Confessions' films in the early seventies. The cinema, opened in 1922, was later taken over by Cannon and then ABC Cinemas before giving up the ghost in 1998 with the arrival of the eight-screen Cineworld multiplex on Old Potts Way.

Potpourri

Ah, yes. The chapter heading that covers all manner of sins. And there are gems here too!

Try, for starters, the third annual Shrewsbury Motor Show in May 1928 at Vincent Greenhous' motor works at Greyfriars. Or Mr Ernest Walton, taking a close look, in 1960, at a 43ft deep well containing human bones and pottery at St Winefride's Convent.

There's a nice shot of Shrewsbury Railway Station in the mid-1950s when the buffet was known as the refreshment rooms. Ahhhh. We rather like that. Here you could get a Double Diamond beer for a mere 1s 7d. Or a brandy for 2s 6d.

We also have some truly striking pictures of Lord Hill's Column, an evocative railway scene from Shrewsbury's last day of steam, swans on the river, Hercules in The Quarry, the Bertram Mills Circus parading into town, the unveiling of the Shropshire War Memorial in 1922, more archaeological digs, more long-gone buildings – and beautiful Shrewsbury in the snow.

When Shrewsbury's head post office closed in November 1959 it moved to a little hut just round the corner. The old building, which was built in 1875, was being demolished and workmen were busy moving fixtures and fittings to the hut.

The interior of Coleham Pumping Station in September 1968. A recording was made this year of the workings of the machinery, and was sold in shops. The steam engines continued to work until November 1970, when electricity took over. The steam engines remained in situ.

Is it a school? Is it a pub? Confused? You would have been. It's 1965 and a brewery company spokesman was promising to take a look at the positioning of a sign outside the Belvidere pub. The sign was causing concern to the headmaster of Belvidere Boys' Secondary Modern School, Mr James Hodgson. The pub sign was standing only six feet from the driveway entrance to the school. 'Anyone driving down the road could be excused for thinking the school is a public house,' said Mr Hodgson.

On 11 January 1965, a goods train ploughed into a signal box at Coton Hill, killing the signalman. The train driver was seriously hurt.

An ammunition train crashed at Shrewsbury station just before 5am on 12 June 1970. The train was hauling empty chlorine tankers and about 50 tons of 120mm tank shells in ammunition trucks, and was pulling into the south end of the station when it hit a parcels train being shunted in the same direction out of a siding at Abbey Foregate. The driver of the ammunition train leapt clear before the collision and was only slightly hurt. Luckily there was no fire after the crash.

Work begins on felling some of the famous limes in The Quarry in April 1945. The limes were considered to be unsafe through age and decay. All the old trees were being removed and the avenues were being replanted. In the early stages of the work about 30 of the more dangerous trees were felled.

Timber! One of the trees comes crashing down, watched by a handful of onlookers in the background.

By February 1952 the last avenue of trees had met its fate. This picture shows one of the last trees to be felled. They were felled using a special procedure. A trench would be dug round the tree and the spreading roots near the surface were cut. Then a steel cable was attached some way up the tree, and it would be pulled over by the winch on a tractor. In this way there was no tree stump left.

On the site of a Saxon king's palace this 43ft deep well, containing human bones and pottery, was discovered by workmen at St Winefride's Convent in 1960. Mr Ernest Walton takes a close look.

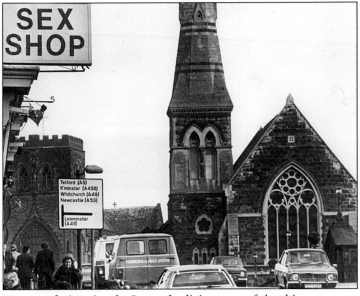

More confusing signals. Sex and religion, two of the things you are never supposed to discuss in pubs for fear of violence breaking out, compete for your attention in this shot across the English Bridge.

The sword is mighty... and in this unusual 1956 picture by *Express & Star* photographer John Rea, it looks as if George Houton is wielding it. But in fact the sword belongs to stony-faced Lord Hill on the top of the 100ft high Lord Hill's Column. Steeplejack George was putting wire netting in place to prevent crumbling masonry falling on the heads of passers-by.

The man in this striking picture is Mr Tom Davies, caretaker, who had the task of cleaning the 172 steps inside Lord Hill's Column. The column, one of Shrewsbury's great landmarks, was built in 1814-16 to commemorate the achievements of Lord Hill in the Peninsular War. This picture was published in 1958. A follow-up story read: 'Archimedes would have loved this,' said Mr Harold Fletcher, when he looked at this photograph in the *Express & Star*. A headmaster with a joy in mathematics, Mr Fletcher was referring to the photograph of the spiral staircase inside Lord Hill's Column. He said: 'This is the finest mathematical picture I have ever seen.' He intended to use copies in lectures to teachers in this country and abroad.

A father and son team have been just about the most daring beauticians in the business (reads the caption for this 1967 picture). Mr George Harris and his son, also George, had made 10 trips a day up and down the 172 steps to his Lordship's perch for the last five weeks. They had completely remodelled Lord Hill's face, including an improved head of hair. George Junior is pictured with Robin Denton of Shrewsbury who had been helping.

Where's he gone? Strange things happen when photographers use wide angle lenses. Lord Hill seems to have vanished from the top of his column in 1968, but it's all an illusion.

The third annual Shrewsbury Motor Show in May 1928 at Vincent Greenhous' motor works at Greyfriars. At the time the firm sold American vehicles – Buicks and Chevrolets.

The Shelton Hospital fire in February 1968 was one of the worst in Shropshire's history. It was discovered at midnight and firemen from all over the county were called, but patients at the psychiatric hospital were choked in their beds by dense smoke. The final death toll was 24.

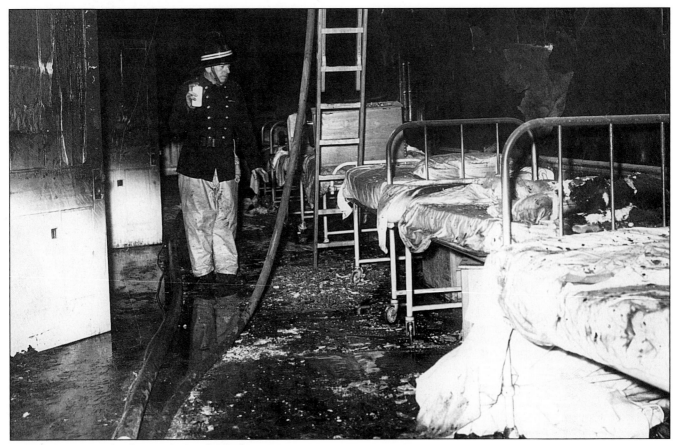

A fireman surveys the damage in Beech Ward.

The buffet at Shrewsbury Railway Station in the mid-1950s. In those days the buffet was known as the refreshment rooms. The young man at the counter near the door is Richard Griffiths, a railway worker, and the servicemen are probably going to RAF Cosford or RAF Bridgnorth. Close inspection reveals some interesting prices – Double Diamond is 1s 7d, port 2s, rum 1s 10d, and brandy 2s 6d.

For generations Shrewsbury was one of Britain's most important railway centres with a fantastically busy station and a huge complex of locomotive sheds shared by friendly rivals: the Great Western Railway and the London Midland and Scottish Railway. The lines radiated out from the station, intersecting the suburbs before heading into open countryside. Here we see Shrewsbury's last day of steam on 4 March 1967, with the locomotive *Clun Castle* hauling a special passenger train into Shrewsbury. The train approaches a crowd of enthusiasts as it snakes past the Severn Bridge signal box, one of the largest of its kind in Europe and described by experts as 'a cathedral among signal boxes'.

A line of cottage chimney pots in Frankwell challenge the dominance of two of the town's beautiful churches, St Alkmund's Church spire (left) and St Julian's tower.

The Welsh Bridge was examined to discover what effects floods had had on the structure in the late 1940s or early 1950s. Here the diver gets ready…

...and here he gets to work, his position betrayed by his helmet breaking surface.

Jack Keech was in a tizzy in 1972 when signs went up describing the county town's alleys as 'shuts'. As the licensee of the Plough, he was not amused when the sign 'Plough Shut' went up near his pub.

The statue of Hercules in The Quarry has been subjected to various indignities over the years, being daubed with paint being one of the lesser crimes against his person. In November 1969 members of the Priory Boys' School Combined Cadet Force gave him a clean. At work are Lance Corporal Glen Ralphs and Cadets Andrew Turner and Keith Turner.

Children take a tip from the swans and find a cool spot underneath the Welsh Bridge in the summer of 1947.

This 'concrete cheese' was causing quite a stir in November 1954, because nobody wanted to pay to get rid of the wartime relic at The Mount. It was the pedestal for a spigot mortar called a Blacker Bombard used by the Home Guard. The gentleman having a close look is Mr A. Cookson. The original 1954 caption describes it as being at 42 The Mount, but Mr Mike Smith of Shrewsbury remembers that when he bought 18 The Mount around 1974 or 1975 it was there in the garden. It was in the way and he broke it up with a pneumatic drill.

Child actor John Howard Davies, who played the title role in the 1948 film *Oliver Twist*, looks up at the Charles Darwin statue in Shrewsbury in 1949. He was in the town to make a personal appearance to promote the movie, which started its run at the Granada on 31 January. Later the youngster became a television director of such shows as *Monty Python*.

A busy scene outside Shrewsbury railway station in the 1940s.

Extensive excavations were planned by Shropshire archaeologists following demolition works in 1972 when a section of
Shrewsbury's medieval defences was revealed. The demolition
of premises on the west side of Pride Hill provided the chance
for excavation and record-taking by members of the
Shropshire Archaeological Society working under the auspices
of the Department of the Environment. Working on the wall is
Mr W.E. Jenks.

The unveiling of the Shropshire War Memorial on 29 July 1922.

Just a few bubbles on the surface mark the spot where the diver is working on the riverbed near Porthill Bridge in March 1966. He was laying a cable which would help reinforce the supply for the Kingsland area. It extended from a sub-station near the multi-storey car park to Woodfield Road. MEB men hauled the cable across the river and the diver covered it on the riverbed with cement bags to prevent it suffering damage.

In October 1973 the go-ahead was given for skeletons found during an archaeological dig in Water Lane, Shrewsbury, to be sent for detailed laboratory examination. Looking at one of Shrewsbury's most important historical finds are Shrewsbury Technical College students with Mr Michael Pitman from Shrewsbury Borough Museum, who is holding a skull.

The funeral of Constable Henry George Andrew Speake at Shrewsbury cemetery on 6 August 1937. Constable Speake, who at 21 was one of the youngest members of the Borough force, died in the River Severn near Uffington. Speake, who was said to be a good swimmer, had gone into the river in pursuit of a 16-year-old boy who had absconded. The inquest heard he had run three quarters of a mile before entering the river and the shock caused heart failure. Many people lined the town streets to watch the funeral procession.

A view from the market hall in the summer of 1967.

A prisoner staged an 11-hour protest among the chimney stacks at Shrewsbury Jail on 5 June 1969. The 24-year-old, serving three years for burglary, ran away from his escort and clambered on the roof. Throughout the protest he talked to a small group of bystanders complaining about conditions, before coming down voluntarily.

This is Bellstone in the 1920s with the National Provincial Bank of England dominating the scene. Next door is Deakin and Son, confectioners.

Although there are no flowers to be seen, this picture of 17-year-old Pamela Walley, on the right, and Barbara Long was taken on the occasion of a Flower Day run by insurance brokers Brentnall Beard and Co on St Johns Hill in about 1955. Girl employees tied and sold bunches of flowers to local insurance brokers to raise money for charity. Pamela, who is now Mrs Pam Sayer, recalls that her bosses Ted and Fred Beard were in the animal guises.

Children play outside Bicton Village Hall in 1974.

March 1949 and a view of Old St Chad's Church.

In its time, says the original caption to this picture, this pillar has been just about as active as the man it commemorates. The memorial to celebrated surgeon William James Clement was originally sited on the forecourt of the railway station but was moved to the Dingle in The Quarry in 1897 and later to St Julian's Friars on the approaches to The Quarry. This is a 1972 photograph.

It is 1961 and children enjoy the peace of the River Severn with the spires of Shrewsbury in the background. But all would soon change, because this was the site of the proposed extension of the Shrewsbury link road which would join the suburbs of Monkmoor and Ditherington with a new bridge. The stretch of road would become known as Telford Way.

A house in Severn Street, Castlefields, soon to be demolished, is inspected here by Shrewsbury MP Sir John Holt and Mr George Paget, residents' association treasurer, in January 1974. The two were touring the Castlefields development area to see what progress had been made. It is something of a miracle, taking into account the redevelopment of that time, that so many of Castlefields' wonderful and fascinating Victorian streets have survived.

A gorgeous winter wonderland dominated by the English Bridge and the famous spires of Shrewsbury in 1952.

The Bertram Mills Circus parade passes close to the railway station in 1962 or 1963. The big top was behind the old Atlas Foundry at Frankwell. The boy on the right is Tony Carter.

William Jenks, a member of the team of Shropshire archaeologists, working with his daughter Sally at the Sutton Farm estate in 1965.

The cobbled approach to the Mardol end of the old Welsh Bridge – also known as St George's Bridge – between Gethin's Garage and the Hill's Arms pub in 1949. The old bridge was demolished in the 1790s. This area was cleared when Smithfield Road was widened and a riverside garden now occupies the site.